Made in United States
Troutdale, OR
12/03/2023

15279220R00070